This journal belongs to

Me

To my on mom

𝓙𝓸𝓾𝓻𝓷𝓪𝓵𝓼 𝓽𝓸 𝓦𝓻𝓲𝓽𝓮 𝓘𝓷

Special Interests Publishing

SUGAR LAND, TEXAS

Journals to Write In

Special Interests Publishing
Sugar Land, Texas
www.sipub.com

Ordering Information:
Quantity sales.
Special discounts are available on quantity purchases by corporations, associations, and others. For details, contact the "Special Sales Department" at the address above.

Was trying to wait until
NY to start this but I
can't sleep so here it
goes. Great time at TSO
& Rota tonight but sat
next to ne...erty &
John. Saw cardinal
@ cabin. I can't sleep
& I'm. It's been a long
night. I can't stand
not being in his life
110%. I know he loves
me & wants a future
but it's almost like
the ~~kids~~ Kids are the
commitment???? I'm scared
I'll screw it up before
he's ready, like being
apart for NYE, his Bday,
my Bday & holidays. →

mon, give me the strength
to get thee because if
we do, life will be
over the top outstanding!
Til the next time ♡

1-1-19 Day 1 of the New Year.
New Years was not what
I wanted it to be but
I went by Kim + Rich/
girls came. I missed
Jake so much, my
life seems to fall
apart when he's gone.
I believe it's because
I don't hear from him
so I feel I don't matter!
This has been a rough
few days, he left this
morning and won't be back
til Wed after work.

Will he ever fight for
me too? I know the kids
come first but its like
2 different lives.
One here w/ me and one
when he picks up the
kids and then I feel
like I don't exist.
I wish the kids:
- Knew about me
- Knew John lived here
Of course I want to
meet them, but I know
John needs time!
I love him and our life
so much! I hope you're
watching and guiding
me so I don't mess
everything up. I don't
know how to live this life
without you

how do I do things alone?
how do I make the right
choices?
There are things I can't
even look 5 you cry
I'm scared!
I Pino mi mama ♡

2/10 mom, I know I haven't written in a long time, but things have been OK until 2 weeks ago. Callen got in the middle and now I'm not going to Abby's bday and Johns movies suck. I'm sure hes scared but hes pushing me away and of course I'm saying all the wrong things and I'm afraid I've done it this time but I'm hurt and I deserve to speak my mind too! I'm sure you're watching and thinking how I'm fucking everything up. I just want to know he needs me like I need him and I don't think he needs me.
I've tried really hard to

make things work w Anthony but that's not working either. He likes to tell me what to do and order him, I don't take it well. The whole thing came out last night and hes a real asshole. You didn't raise us this way. The 5,000 you lent him, he doesn't feel he owes me anything. He can take the girls on vacation and go away & ??? but always complains about it. He wouldn't go to the Hawks game for my b-day but could go down for hers b-day.

I have so many hard feelings towards him and I guess can't get past it.

It started to effect and then when you were sick and he wants me out of the house cuz he wants this. He has no idea how hard this is for me. Jada gets it but I'm afraid I've lost him. If I have, its only my fault.

I don't know how to do this life w/o you. As I look to the future, I see a very lonely person and it's all me.

I wish you had done your will or something so that part would have been easier but you left us in a bind and I'm tired of arguing and fighting and crying

I want to be my strong, happy person again but I don't know how to get her back, she might be gone for good.

I need to find someone to talk to and these are my priorities:

1. Getting myself back
2. John if he'll have me
3. Work
4. House
5. Anything's

John takes care of me and puts up a lot of shit, I just want to be part of his life too. Things were great but there's a breakdown when

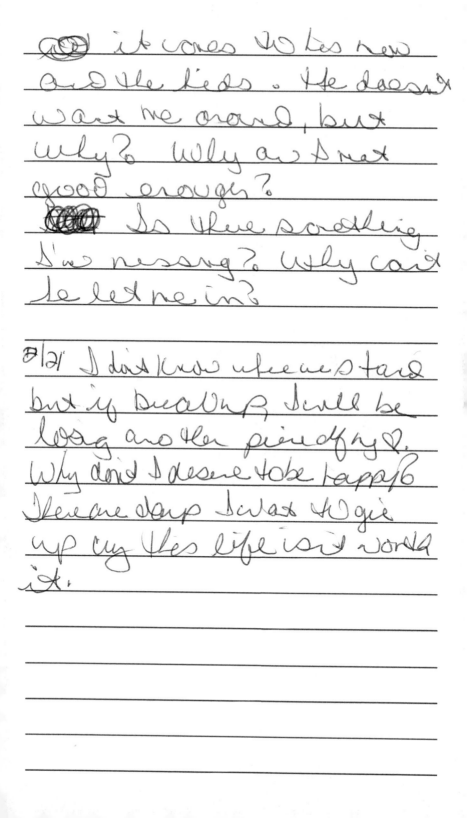

~~○○~~ it comes to his new and the kids. He doesn't want me around, but why? Why am I not good enough?

~~●●●~~ Is there something I'm missing? Why can't he let me in?

8/21 I don't know where we stand but if breaking I will be losing another piece of my ♥. Why don't I deserve to be happy? There are days I want to give up my this life isn't worth it.

2/25

New start, blank page
Had to deal c my car today)
I don't need more issues
I just need to heal.

2/26 Long day @ work,
feeling caught up, great
meeting c Br Jennings.
Chris helped fix my car
+ Dave met $

2/27 "Work from home"
much needed. Stay in
PJ's Pdo mo thing.
cancelled girls dinner
dly tired, pain, sinus
pressure.
     So John just picked
up his things. How do
u love someone but
walk away? :-)

Steven said I have to
focus on my man + kids.
I get it but then what
an I?
My heart is broke
my life is broken
why does Chis want
to help me?

3/5 Told Chas we can't
could to see each other
so much as its getting
to confy

3/6 missing man + kids.
why has life changed so
much, I just want to be
happy

3/8 Nice night in my PJs
o wine + a movie. Its
very hard being alone. I
dont know how to do this

3/9 Out o friends/family
for St Pattys Day bar
crawl. I had so much
fun but its hard putting
on a happy face.

July 4 - Its been awile but life has been ok. Does of nothing dates but thats ok. At least I know what I want + dont.
Its time for a new job -- -- --

Aug - Started talking to this guy but hes lazt + caled, Kinda weird. Time will tell.

Aug 4 - My B-day was weird + caled. Terry blew me off again, So I'm done c̄ that.

Sept 11 - Out c̄ my cousin Sandy today - Girls pamping And a date later c̄ the guy for ealier

There we go again, he blew me off. Why do I have such bad luck?

Aug 12. OK he's coming over, Lee to work last night

Aug 13: What great, he's so easy to talk to and we were very attracted to each other.

Oct 11 = Its 2 months -
Insisted in a Happy
Anniversary + all I got
was a Thank you.

- Forgot about Shopping
Oct 6 we went Shopping
for clothes for Larissa's
Wedding Oct 12.

- We watched Bears games,
I'm disappointed I can't
get him to watch the
Hawks - he even once,
and no mention of really
friends + family.
When I was in those
he met Sandy/Raj, Rita,
Rino, DC/um + the new
Larissa + everyone at the
wedding.

Oct 17-18

The argument last night
was bad, I slept 2 hours
and ended up sleeping
most of the day.
Hurtful things were said,
why don't I matter? Why
don't my thoughts or feelings
matter? Why have we
never gone on a date?

I'm laying here thinking about what was said tonight and theres truth to some and not to others. As far as tues night, I turned never turn my back to you you were snoring. I kissed you like I usually do and rolled over. I sleep on my side as I hv seen you've noticed, just like you sleep on your stomach.

There has been something on my mind but please know, You're my person, the person I text and look forward to talking too and confiding in. I see a future, even if it looks foggy to you.

When what you see as
shutting down has been on
my mind about 3 weeks
but I was scared because
of us. Because of not
knowing what I say to you.
I've enjoyed you meeting friends
and family and want you
to meet more but I don't
know why I'm not part of
your life. I noticed watching
the Bears game that night
and was shut down, yes
she says hello and wants
pictures of the wedding
but when I mentioned her
tonight, you were silent.
When you were going by
Sydney, I wanted to go
and was told no. I
understand the reasons
behind both situations

But this never been t all
of meeting anyone.
When were together, I can block
everything out. I love hearing
about your crazy work and
how much you love it. I
love hearing about what
made you ... you. I get lost
in your eyes and love your
touch. Having sex and
making love is beyond
amazing. When I say I
miss you, its not to make
you feel bad, its because
I do miss you, even if
its a day. I feel connected
to you. You make me happy.
I smile the biggest
I ever have when around me
around you. The one thing
that should bring us closer
is tearing us apart. I love you,

Made in the USA
Lexington, KY
16 November 2018